LEISURE IN A DEMOCRACY

T0345941

NATIONAL BOOK LEAGUE SIXTH ANNUAL LECTURE

LEISURE IN A DEMOCRACY

VISCOUNT SAMUEL

LONDON

PUBLISHED FOR THE

NATIONAL BOOK LEAGUE

BY THE CAMBRIDGE UNIVERSITY PRESS

1949

CAMBRIDGE
UNIVERSITY PRESS

University Printing House, Cambridge CB2 8BS, United Kingdom

Cambridge University Press is part of the University of Cambridge.

It furthers the University's mission by disseminating knowledge in the pursuit of education, learning and research at the highest international levels of excellence.

www.cambridge.org
Information on this title: www.cambridge.org/9781107494718

© Cambridge University Press 1949

First published 1949
Re-issued 2015

A catalogue record for this publication is available from the British Library

ISBN 978-1-107-49471-8 Paperback

LEISURE IN A DEMOCRACY

I

THE nineteenth century had a poor opinion of the eighteenth; and no doubt, on the whole, its strictures were justified. Yet there was a certain atmosphere about the eighteenth century which we in these days may recall with some regret, even with a little envy. The England of the Vicar of Wakefield and Jane Austen; the London of Canaletto; Georgian architecture and gardens, furniture and pictures, and silver in the candle-light; the prose of Addison and Steele and Gibbon, the poetry of Gray and Cowper; families on Sundays, tranquil and neatly dressed, walking along the footpaths decently to Church—we look around us, and we feel there is something that we are missing.

That way of life could not last. There came the French Revolution, the Terror, the Marseillaise; the armies of Napoleon sweeping over Europe—at one moment poised menacingly close there at Boulogne. *La carrière ouverte aux talents*; also freedom of thought—opportunity open to ideas. There came science, invention, machines, and the Industrial Revolution: vast, shapeless factory towns, hastily built; millions of working-people, early in the morning, late in the evening, crowding in and out of the gates of the mills, mines, ironworks, shipyards. Afterwards came the Second Industrial Revolution—with electricity, chemical processes, the internal combustion engine, motor-cars and airplanes. And now we hear the first rumblings of the Third Industrial Revolution, destined perhaps to be even more subversive than either of the others, tapping for man's service the primal energy of the universe.

5

We draw breath and look around us, and we are aware of the kind of civilization that we have. We find in this island six times as many people living as there were in the middle of the eighteenth century. We find cramped homes, congested cities, rush-hour travel, hurry and strain; nature crowded out. As Emerson said:

> Things are in the saddle
> And ride mankind.

2

The price we have paid is heavy, but let us remember that we have bought much that is of value. Science and the machines have greatly lightened the burden of brute labour, mankind's oppressor all through the ages. For less toil they have given us the things that we need in a variety and an abundance undreamt of till now. The advantage of this greater production of wealth could be disbursed in a choice of ways. It might have gone mainly to the capitalist employers, in larger profits; or to the workmen, in higher wages and shorter hours; or to the consumers, in larger supplies and lower prices. Or the State might lay hands on it by heavier taxation, and spend it on wars, or on social equipment and amenities. Or it might have been distributed among several of these objects, or, as in fact it was, among all of them.

Simultaneously with the First Industrial Revolution, and partly as a consequence of it, came in this country the rise of democracy. It favoured the use of the rapidly growing output of industry in remedying the worst of the social evils which, in the earlier half of the nineteenth century, still afflicted the mass of the people. Fifty years ago, when my generation was young, we had still to devote our political energies to attacking the sweated wages, excessive hours, insecurity of livelihood, slum housing, scanty education, which were the scandal of the time. Though checked and thwarted by two ruinous wars and the disastrous economic depression between, the sustained efforts to that end have to a great extent succeeded. A national minimum has been established. Destitution is almost unknown. We no longer hear of the problem of "the submerged tenth". The younger generation of today, preparing to take over in its turn, finds itself, in the middle of the twentieth century, dealing with a population at a far higher economic and cultural level than had been reached at the beginning. Undoubtedly here and there some of the old defects and deficiencies remain—conspicuously in the matter of housing: and these still have a first claim on our energies. But, viewing the situation as a whole, we see our society relieved, in large degree, from the heavy pressure of urgent material needs. It can turn more of its attention to the immaterial. We must still ensure a supply of "things", and abundantly: but we need no longer allow them to "ride mankind". Wisely the community decides to devote a larger share of the growing usufruct of productive power to lessening the proportion of men's lives that is devoted to earning the means of living, and in increasing the proportion given to the enjoyment of life itself. And the life is more than the livelihood, the workman more than the work. In a word, the community can be more active now in enlarging leisure and the opportunities for the right use of it. That is the theme of my Address to you today.

3

The problems that face us in this new field are vast. The actual amount of leisure already available has been expanded quite suddenly of late, and that has greatly increased the difficulties, already serious, in handling the situation. Mark how many have been the recent changes that have contributed to this.

The years devoted to what is officially called "gainful occupation" have been shortened at both ends. The school age has been raised, to the general advantage. At the same time retirement is earlier, while longevity is increasing. People begin work later than they used; they leave it sooner; and they live longer after they have left. We have to cater for the leisure of more young people and many more old people. Taking as the criterion the pensionable age of sixty-five for men and sixty for women, we are told that in 1901 there were two-and-a-quarter millions such people in our population: in 1941 the number had risen to five-and-a-half millions: it is estimated that in 1971 it will be about nine-and-a-half millions.[1]

The working-day also is shorter. In my youth a standard eight-hour day was the distant ideal of the more optimistic reformers: now eight hours is established as the usual maximum; in some great industries the rule is seven. Incidentally, the number of hours serviceable for outdoor occupations has been increased by the adoption of Willett's ingenious scheme of time adjustment. He called it Daylight Saving: introducing the Bill to establish it, during the first World War, I had the privilege of acting godfather, and giving it the name, now so familiar, of Summer Time.

The week-end rest too has been lengthened: it had been one day ever since the time of the Ten Commandments: in our own generation it has been made a day and a half; it seems on the way to become two days in the next. Not

[1] As percentages of the population: 1901—6·2 per cent; 1941—12 per cent; 1971—20·8 per cent. (Registrar-General's Figures) *Social Insurance and Allied Services; Report by Sir William Beveridge, 20 Nov. 1942*, Cmd. 6404, H.M. Stationery Office, 1942, 2s.

less important is the lengthening of the annual holiday; now carrying pay for a large proportion of the working population. As a consequence, the number of people for whom provision has to be made in the holiday season has suddenly been doubled. Mr. Butlin, of the Holiday Camps, who knows all about these things, told a recent conference that in 1937 it was fifteen millions, in 1947 thirty millions. In every direction the problem to be dealt with has been vastly enlarged.

The uncomfortable question arises whether we can afford all this. But that is not a matter for discussion on this occasion. If I were speaking to a meeting of politicians or of economists I should have to remind them that we seem to be drawing on the disposable surplus of production in many ways all at once. Shorter hours and longer holidays is only one item. Money-wages are higher. Profits are often excessive. Government expenditure is very large, and taxation remains a heavy burden. All this together is reflected in higher prices: with higher cost of living, higher costs of production, dearer exports to compete in the world markets, and inflationary pressure on the value of sterling. If to all the rest there were added deliberate restrictions upon output—whether by monopolist employers, or by monopolistic trade unions, or, worst of all, by combinations of the two exploiting the general public, then indeed the situation would become impossible. The National Book League, however, would not wish to discuss in detail these questions of economics. None the less, in any survey of leisure these are considerations not to be left out of account.

There is still one more factor that comes in to complicate our problem even further. At the very time that leisure has so greatly increased, and the need for opportunities to use it rightly has so rapidly expanded, the resources that were available in earlier times have contracted as rapidly.

9

Patronage is disappearing. Literature, the drama and music, architecture, painting and sculpture, sports and games as well, had depended, all through the centuries, largely on patronage. Kings, princes and nobles, the Church and the universities, City corporations, guilds, wealthy merchants, accepted the duty to encourage them, and made it their pride. Now these sources have dwindled or vanished altogether. Power has passed from their hands and taxation has crippled their capacities. Here and there new benefactors appear, subsidizing movements or establishing Foundations with great generosity. But this goes only a little way towards meeting so great a need. Democracy cannot expect, and does not expect, both to supersede the wealthy and to continue to rely on their help. It must rely upon itself—that is upon the multitude. The problem before us in these times is how to organize and mobilize the multitude to do what used to be done in their heyday by powerful nobles and wealthy corporations.

4

Faced by a task such as this, people are often inclined first to ask what the Government is doing about it. What new legislation is needed? Ought we to have a Minister of Fine Arts, as in France? Or even, as one of our legislators recently suggested in a newspaper article, a Minister of Pleasure? State action is conspicuous, understood by everyone, easily publicized: attention is liable to be focussed on it. But in this case that would clearly be to begin at the wrong end. It is the individual, his ideas, his tastes, that matter most. Since it is leisure in a democracy that we are discussing, and not in a Fascist, Nazi or Communist society, we accept from the outset that the spending of his own leisure should depend upon the choice, the action of the individual himself. The State may encourage and enable; it must not impose. Public opinion may suggest, persuade, lead; it must not drive. A regulated leisure is a contradiction in terms.

The individual may at times prefer to idle. If he does not carry it too far, he may be quite right. "I loaf and invite my soul", said Walt Whitman. And Barrie wrote: "You must have been warned against letting the golden hours slip by. Yes, but some of them are golden only because we let them slip". And Wordsworth:

> To sit without emotion, hope, or aim,
> In the loved presence of my cottage fire,
> And listen to the flapping of the flame,
> Or kettle whispering its faint undersong.

In childhood and youth, and to a great extent in adult life, the use of leisure is conditioned by the character of the home. Straightway we are brought back to the housing problem. A boy or girl, one of a family packed into a little flat, with no chance of privacy, no room for hobbies or quiet reading, is under a terrible handicap during the formative years. For the woman's half of the community the home is more often the enemy of leisure than its friend. This has become so increasingly in recent years. There is no statistic that can measure the economic loss to the nation, as well as the personal frustration, through the waste of the time of intensively trained and highly qualified women on petty domestic tasks that could be done as well by a less valuable grade of worker. Cabinet Ministers or Civil Servants would rightly refuse to be deprived of their clerks and secretaries. The trade unions would never allow the skill of the artisan to be wasted on labourer's work. We shall not have taken seriously the right organization of the opportunities for leisure until, first, the homes of the people are large enough to allow some privacy for the members of a family, and some room for friendly conversation and entertainment; and secondly, until they can be so staffed as to relieve housewives of their present often exhausting burdens.

So far as may be, it is for the town or neighbourhood to make good the deficiencies of the home. This is now recognized. Society accepts it as its duty to see that the urban environment is properly planned; with sufficient playgrounds, rest-gardens, playing-fields, green belts or green wedges; and provided with community centres, health centres, public halls, libraries. Voluntary organizations take part, promoting all kinds of clubs and associations—athletic, social, musical, dramatic, political, industrial. Many of these voluntary organizations are national in their scope—the Arts Council, the National Trust, Societies concerned with planning, rambling, Youth Hostels, and holiday accommodation of all kinds. Commercial enterprises take part, as of old—theatres, cinemas, concerts, dance-halls. New ones are formed to cater for the expanding needs. The Butlin Camps, for example, found holiday accommodation in the 1948 season, in relays, for half a million people.

Now as to the State. It is long since it entered this field. It passed much valuable legislation in the course of years —enacting the Bank Holidays; establishing museums, galleries, libraries, public baths; securing early closing in the shops; shortening the hours of labour in industries; requiring holidays with pay; planning the towns and protecting the countryside. The work is actively going forward. In the present parliamentary session a Bill is to be passed to establish national parks and nature reserves and to protect the amenities of the coast-line. Funds are being allocated, and a site provided, for a National Theatre. Preparations are in hand for a cultural Festival in 1951 as a centennial of the Great Exhibition.

After this brief survey of the present situation and the causes that have led to it I shall turn to the prospects for the future, and submit one or two suggestions for your consideration. But before doing so I would draw your attention to two dangers that attach to State activity in the cultural field.

The first is that the State, while bringing help, may insist upon direction. We have seen, in Italy, in Germany and in Russia, how real this danger is and how disastrous it may prove. Nothing is more highly individualistic than the genius of the artist, and so it must remain. Art may be "made tongue-tied by Authority", as Shakespeare says. Not long ago, in a lecture to the Fabian Society discussing these matters,[1] Mr. Priestley said: "The artist wonders rather dubiously about the Socialist atmosphere of co-operation, committees and common sense; asks himself how he will like it when splendid wealthy patrons are replaced by earnest and dreary town councillors". Happily, in this country the danger is realized, all the more fully now, with the object-lesson before us of the experience of our European neighbours. State grants to the Universities have been greatly increased, but the independence of the Universities is respected as scrupulously as before. Government controls broadcasting, but does not seek to direct it. Many useful voluntary organizations are being subsidized, but without being made subordinate. This is sound policy, which the nation is likely to insist should be maintained.

The second danger is more actual. It is that the advent of democracy, and the substitution of public for private patronage, may lead to a lowering of standards.

[1] *The Arts under Socialism*, Turnstile Press, 1947, 1s.

The French Revolution, in reaction from the flaunted luxury of the *ancien régime*, produced the *sans-culottes*. We have had no social revolution and nothing of the same kind here. But we may have noticed sometimes in recent years a strange fashion, away on the left—a kind of inverted snobbery: slovenly clothes, slipshod speech, off-hand manners, offered as proof of the proletarian sincerity of the converted highbrow. However, such tendency as there has been of that kind now seems to be fading away. The turning-point may have been reached this year, when a Labour Government has revived the old ceremonial at the opening of the Parliamentary Session, that had been in abeyance for ten years—the King, in presence of the two Houses, crowned, robed and enthroned; the Queen, as from a fairy-tale; the peers in their mediaeval robes of crimson and ermine. I think it showed wisdom to revive it. This pageantry does no one harm; it derogates from the liberties of no man: but by enhancing the prestige and dignity, it strengthens the stability and authority of the State, in which every man is a member. Mr. Gladstone once said to a supporter of his in the House of Commons, who, years afterwards, told it to me, "I hate luxury but I love splendour".

In Britain the reaction from the luxury of the sixteenth-, seventeenth- and eighteenth-century aristocrats was not a spectacular and savage revolution, but the drab puritanism of the public and private life of the nineteenth. A mature democracy has now grown beyond that. Seeking to bring liberty and happiness into the lives of the whole people, it favours brightness, colour, music, play. A democracy may be strong and effective without being dull. It may aim at a classless society and gradually establish it, and yet, at the same time, carry forward and include within itself all that was fine in the old aristocracy —the grace of culture, the beauty of art. And if it succeeds in finding and advancing the best among the whole body of its members to be its own governors and leaders, if also it can bring the whole body to accept their standards of what is seemly and right to be done, then the modern democracy may itself become a new aristocracy, and nobler than any that the past has known.

6

From these levels let us come back again now to the immediate and the practical. How are these general ideas to be applied, here and now?

We start once more with the individual. Here it is again a question of opportunities. The young are blamed for not putting their leisure to good use, and sometimes falling into bad ways as a consequence—preferring to watch other people playing games rather than play them themselves; reading no books; letting their school education fall into disrepair; the great majority joining no clubs or movements; finding their amusements in "Fun Fairs", football pools, murder stories and gangster films. But consider, before you pass a general condemnation, what little chance very many of them have for anything better. Games: is there a playing-field within reach?—reading: where can they read with four or five people in a home of two or three rooms?—interesting hobbies: where to practise them?—clubs: are there club-leaders enough to provide them for more than a fraction of all those millions? —murder stories and gangster films: what better ones are offered? The simplest pleasures are still the best, and the most sought after—walking and cycling; outdoor and indoor games; music, dancing and singing; gardening and all the range of hobbies. Let the nation first make these, and the others, possible and easy before blaming the young for neglecting them.

In one point Soviet Russia can set us an example here. Special facilities are given to boys and girls to practise their hobbies—photography, radio, model engines, ships and planes, music, organized games and the like. In Leningrad a former royal palace is used for this purpose, and various buildings in towns and villages all over the country. Inquiry might well be made whether there would be a demand for such facilities here. If there were it should be satisfied, perhaps in connection with Community Centres or young people's clubs.

A leisure occupation, which is found to fit a person's aptitudes and is pursued with zest and success, may develop into his main occupation; from amateur it may become professional, and provide the livelihood. This touches a question of great, indeed of the first importance —how to enable talent and genius to emerge in a democratic State. Mr. Bernard Shaw wrote an article on this not long ago, full of interesting suggestions.[1] He would answer the question by short hours for the bread-and-butter occupation, and the use of leisure for what he terms "voluntary experimental apprenticeship". He reminds us that "Rousseau lived by copying music, Spinoza by grinding lenses, Wagner by conducting (and borrowing), Dickens as a clerk, Wells as a schoolmaster, others as journalists or what not". It is a line of approach well worth pursuing.

We cannot escape depending on the individual as the ultimate arbiter of taste. Progressive architects may design admirable houses, but if the tenants insist upon sham Tudor they are likely to get from the builders what they want. The fine efforts of the Georgian Society to defend what is left of past excellences in Bath, in Hove, in the Regent's Park terraces and elsewhere; the similar efforts of the Preservation Trusts of Oxford, Cambridge and other

[1] *The New Statesman and Nation,* 26 April, 1947.

towns; the magnificent plans for the gradual re-shaping of the London area, the West Midlands, and many of the chief cities throughout the country—these can succeed only if there is a public opinion active in their support. And the public is nothing else than the individual multiplied and aggregated. It is the public also which alone can cure, not only the major vices of our badly-planned urban environment, but also its minor, but still reprehensible bad habits—advertisements, litter, noise, and smoke. That these are not hard to cure the example of Stockholm and other Scandinavian cities proves conclusively.

Industrial design stands on the same footing. Good design is not more costly than bad. It is often less costly; for many bad designs are so because they have aimed at expensiveness for the sake of exclusiveness, instead of at fitness and beauty for their own sake. Here democracy is more likely to do well than plutocracy: for its aim must be to make articles of good design available for every workman's home, and therefore at a low price; it can do this best by concentrating on the beauty of shape, colour and texture rather than upon elaborate adornment. It realizes, as has been well said, that "simplicity is the peak of civilization". The difference is plain to see, here in London, when we compare one of the last examples of plutocratic taste, the Tower Bridge, its sham medievalism and constructed decorations, with the strong clean lines, fit and graceful, of the new Waterloo Bridge, typical of a democratic age at its best.

This vast network of voluntary agencies that cater directly or indirectly for leisure, they too depend upon the action of the individual. To show initiative and take responsibility in forming and maintaining those agencies used to be the function mainly of the leisured class. Now, if the duty is to be done at all, the many must undertake it in their own part-time leisure, since soon there will no longer be any whole-time leisure of a few.

7

We come back to the province of the State. Adult education enters here: it is likely to fill an ever-increasing place in State activities. But that is a subject far too wide to be dealt with incidentally in this discussion, and needs a separate consideration.

For encouraging the arts, extending amenities and safeguarding the standards of taste, new agencies have been established. The Arts Council, with large subventions from the Treasury, is carrying on the admirable work which we watch with so keen an interest. The Royal Fine Arts Commission fulfils great responsibilities in giving guidance, in the province assigned to it, to the Government Departments and other public bodies.

I would venture to make a suggestion of a way, not hitherto adopted in this country, in which State action might usefully be extended. Many good citizens who have accumulated fortunes find it difficult to decide how they can best dispose of them. They may have few family obligations, or none. There may be no cause or movement which interests them sufficiently to make them choose it as their legatee. In the past it was usual for people so situated to leave their money for charitable purposes; but there is no longer the same need for almshouses, apprenticing poor boys, or the like. Hospitals have often been the beneficiaries; with a National Health Service it is doubtful to what extent this will continue. Some make art collections, and then give or bequeath them to their town or to the nation; but the greater part are not connoisseurs, or not so disposed. Few are wealthy enough to endow separate Foundations, like Rockefeller, or Nuffield, or Harkness of the Pilgrim Trust. Now and then we read of someone who has left the residue of his estate to the Chancellor of the Exchequer for reduction of the National Debt; but to most of us that would seem to be, as an excited orator once said, "a mere fleabite in the ocean".

Now in Scotland they have a local institution which bears the fine old title of "The Common Good". It originated in grants of land to the Royal Burghs conferred by the Sovereigns of Scotland in ancient charters. Additions were made later, and modern legislation has brought in other classes of towns. The total sum accumulated from grants, gifts and bequests, standing to the credit of the various burghs, now approaches £4,000,000, with an annual income of over £400,000. This is spent on a variety of purposes—improvements of Corporation property not otherwise provided for; the defence of public interests; "the upholding of the dignity of the burgh"; and "generally, any purpose which in the bona fide judgement of the Town Council is for the good of the community as a whole".[1]

Might we not have a Common Good Statute establishing such Funds on a national basis in England, Scotland and Wales; with local Funds in any boroughs, as already in Scotland, where the Corporation so desires? The central Funds would be vested in National Trustees, the local Funds in the several Corporations. The purposes would be the provision of any kind of public amenity for which money is not already available. The allocation might be modelled on the admirable procedure of the National Trust, the National Art-Collections Fund, the Pilgrim Trust, and other such Foundations; whose own revenues might indeed be supplemented by grants from this new source. The State has set a precedent in establishing the

[1] These particulars have kindly been supplied to me by the Scottish Office.

Department of the Public Trustee, which relieves private persons of the burden of administering estates (now amounting to a value of £500,000,000). It would be extending to public benefactions the system already adopted for private fortunes. And as in that case so in this, the service need cost the taxpayer nothing, the charges being met by a small percentage fee. Once created, and established in the confidence of the public, such Common Good Funds, both central and local, might attract, in the course of generations, very large sums that would otherwise be dissipated ineffectually. They might conduce greatly to the benefit of the community, in ways less conspicuous but not less valuable than those financed by the rates and taxes.

The best refreshment for tired people is often in travel, in their own country or outside it. The action of the State comes in again here; it passes beyond the national sphere into the international. Tourism in our day is perhaps still only in its beginnings. With diffusion of wealth and of education carried further, with longer holidays and more money to pay for them, and especially if air-travel becomes safe and cheap, the number of people making pleasure journeys abroad may be multiplied many times. What use of leisure is more worth while, more to be encouraged?

The obvious first step is to remove the present passport, currency and other restrictions, at the earliest moment that the conditions allow. Many improvements in transport, accommodation and comfort are recognized to be necessary and feasible. Here the Travel Association is doing good work, helped by a large subsidy from the Treasury. The grant is fully justified, even on narrow economic grounds alone; for tourism in Great Britain may soon prove a more effective dollar-earning industry than the export of coal, or textiles, or machinery. Everything that promotes mutual understanding and goodwill among the peoples encourages travel and the interchange of ideas. The British Council plays a most useful part in this, so far as the inadequate funds at its disposal allow. UNESCO, in which we are partners with the other nations, crowns the complex structure of agencies through which our modern civilization seeks to deal with the leisure needs of a democratic world.

8

Three powerful factors, operating over the whole of our field, we have not yet mentioned: one is the newspaper press; the second, broadcasting; the third, books. This is not the occasion on which to discuss the intricacies of the problems of the press. Radio has also become a highly specialized subject. One or two brief observations however may be permitted. As a medium for the dissemination of ideas, radio, in twenty or thirty years, has become as powerful as printing after five centuries. For music it is already doing as much as the printing-press has ever done for literature. The B.B.C. tells us that the average radio audience which listens to a Wednesday evening Symphony Concert broadcast from the Albert Hall would be enough to fill three hundred Albert Halls.

I believe that the public in general is very satisfied with the way in which the managers of the B.B.C. are fulfilling the task, as difficult as it is responsible, entrusted to them. If some of the programmes are below the standards that might be wished that is the fault, not of the producer, but of the consumer; who, as we know, is always right. B.B.C. Listener Research tells us that sixty adults will listen to Saturday Night Music-Hall on the Home Service; compared with about twenty for Questions of the Hour, ten for Promenade Concerts, and one for Symphony Concerts and Plays in the Third Programme. Here we come back again to the responsibility of the individual. If we believe in democratic freedom, the people are entitled to get from a public service what they want to have, and not only what it might desire to give.

It is against this background of a vast comprehensive movement, seeking one aim, the best use of increasing leisure, along many paths and through many agencies, that we should see the work of our National Book League. It permeates all the rest. The pursuit of knowledge and the stimulus of imagination; philosophy, religion and science, history and art, politics and economics, wit and wisdom—where would they all be without books? "Society", said Oliver Wendell Holmes, "is a strong solution of books. It draws its virtue out of what is best worth reading, as hot water draws the strength of tea-leaves". Or we might quote a friend of many of us here, the late Sir Denison Ross, who wrote, with amiable frankness, that "One reads: (1) to study a special subject; (2) to acquaint oneself with a literary classic; (3) to forget troubles; (4) to pass the time; (5) to get to sleep; (6) to be amused; (7) to keep abreast of other people".

The true lover of books is on his guard against being bookish. As Lin Yutang tells us, "the wise man reads both books and life itself". Dr. Johnson said much the same thing: "'This man', said he, gravely, 'was a very sensible man, who perfectly understood common affairs; a man of a great deal of knowledge of the world, fresh from life, not strained through books'". So the National Book League sets out to discourage pedantry, to keep literature in touch with life, and life with literature. It can render no better service to our democracy for its hours of leisure than that.

It is usual to say that we are living in an age of transition. I suppose we always have been. I remember Dean

22

Inge saying, "It is believed that when our first parents left Paradise, Adam turned to Eve and said, 'My dear, we are living in an age of transition'". But our own epoch is unique in this, that it finds itself involved in three great transitions simultaneously: from intuition and guess-work to science; from hand labour to machinery; from the rule of the few to the rule of the many. No wonder that it is difficult to adjust ourselves, that we are tossed about and confused. No wonder that we find it hard to maintain our standards.

When at the beginning of this Address, I recalled the atmosphere of the eighteenth century, tranquil and urbane, and said that we feel now there is something missing—it is just that; it is that the finer standards of aristocracy, using the word in its best sense, are being trodden underfoot in the rough and tumble of democracy. Matthew Arnold gave us the right message when he wrote, "Many are to be made partakers in well-being, true; but the ideal of well-being is not to be, on that account, lowered and coarsened".

Let us keep whatever survives of ease and quiet and comfort; not curtail it, but rather extend it to all. Britain has been the progenitor of a long line, second to none, of great men, illustrious in every sphere of human endeavour. Let us so order our affairs that that may be so still; but, in addition, that Britain may become, what it has never been and is not yet, the home of a people, from top to bottom and through and through, cultured and finely civilized; a nation and its environment with a quality of dignity and grace.

www.ingramcontent.com/pod-product-compliance
Ingram Content Group UK Ltd.
Pitfield, Milton Keynes, MK11 3LW, UK
UKHW020449010325
455719UK00015B/497